SNAPSHOTS IN HISTORY

ASSASSINATION AT SARAJEVO

The Spark That Started World War I

by Robin S. Doak

ASSASSINATION AT SARAJEVO

The Spark That Started World War I

by Robin S. Doak

Content Adviser: Steve Remy, Ph.D.,
Associate Professor of History, Brooklyn College and
Graduate Center, City University of New York

Reading Adviser: Katie Van Sluys, Ph.D.,
School of Education, DePaul University

Compass Point Books ✦ Minneapolis, Minnesota

◈ Compass Point Books

151 Good Counsel Drive
P.O. Box 669
Mankato, MN 56002-0669

 This book was manufactured with paper containing
at least 10 percent post-consumer waste.

For Compass Point Books
Brenda Haugen, XNR Productions, Inc., Catherine Neitge,
Keith Griffin, Ashlee Suker, LuAnn Ascheman-Adams, and Nick Healy

Produced by White-Thomson Publishing Ltd.
For White-Thomson Publishing
Stephen White-Thomson, Susan Crean, Amy Sparks,
Tinstar Design Ltd., Tom Lansford, Peggy Bresnick Kendler,
and Timothy Griffin

Library of Congress Cataloging-in-Publication Data
Doak, Robin S. (Robin Santos), 1963–
  Assassination at Sarajevo : the spark that started World War I / by
Robin S. Doak.
      p. cm. — (Snapshots in history)
  Includes bibliographical references and index.
  ISBN 978-0-7565-3857-6 (library binding)
  1. Franz Ferdinand, Archduke of Austria, 1863–1914—
Assassination—Juvenile literature. 2. Austria—History—Franz
Joseph I, 1848–1916—Juvenile literature. 3. World War, 1914–
1918—Causes—Juvenile literature. I. Title. II. Series.
  DB89.F7D63 2008
  940.3'11—dc22   2008007545

Visit Compass Point Books on the Internet at
www.compasspointbooks.com
or e-mail your request to
custserv@compasspointbooks.com

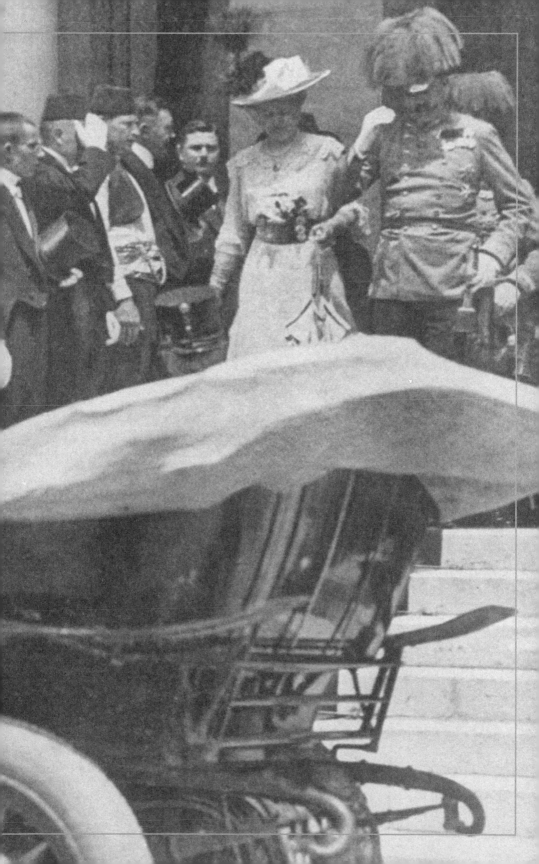

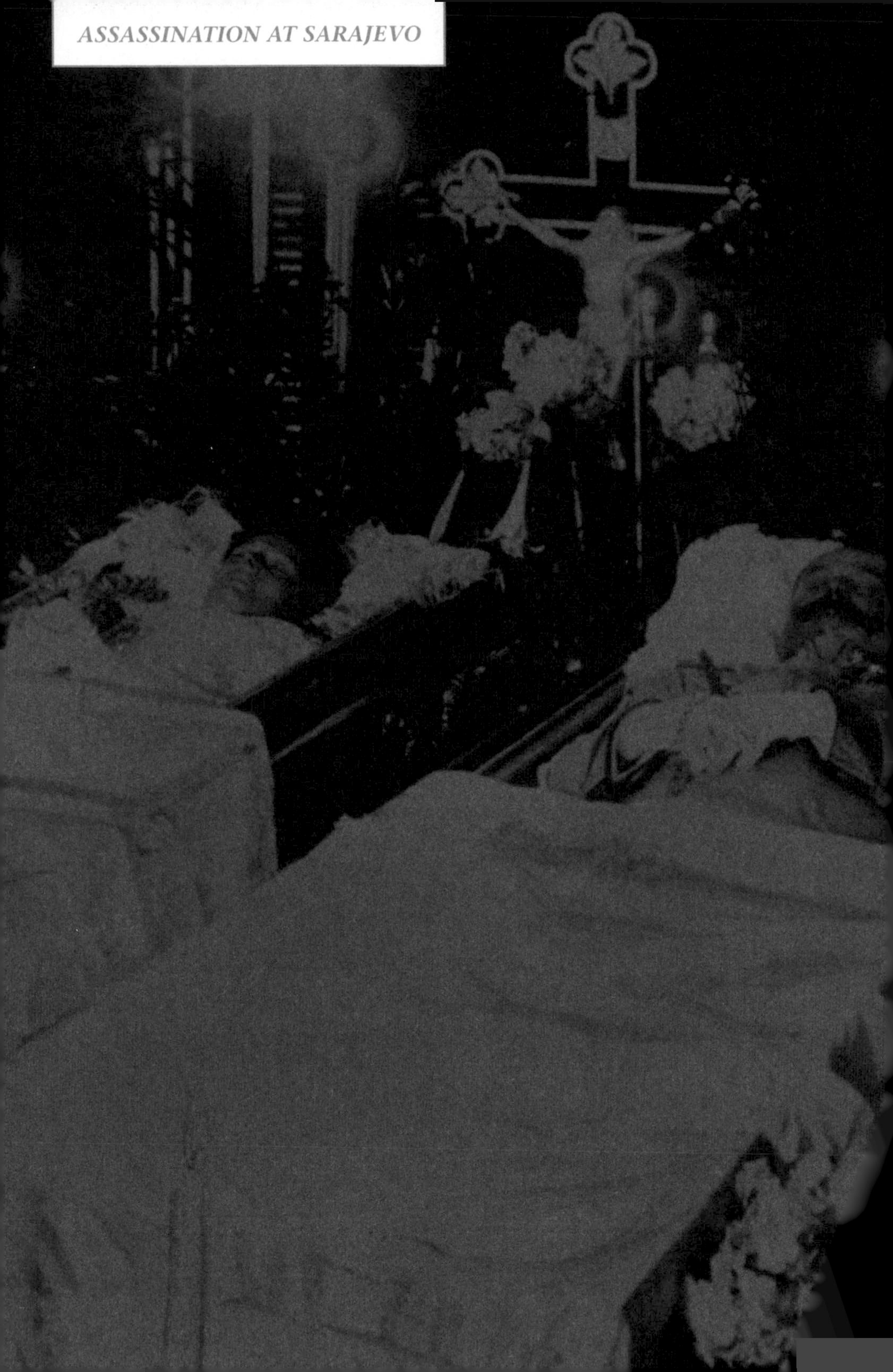

CONTENTS

Public Assassination

Archduke Franz Ferdinand and his wife, Sophie, sat quietly in the open car as it rolled through the streets of Sarajevo, a city in the Balkan province of Bosnia and Herzegovina. The crowds lining the streets cheered and waved to the royal couple. But lurking among the welcoming spectators was a killer waiting for his chance to strike.

It was June 28, 1914, and the clouds and rain of the last few days had given way to warm, sunny weather in the province commonly known as Bosnia. Pictures of Franz Ferdinand, the future emperor of Austria-Hungary, were displayed in many windows, and colorful flags and rugs hung from others in a welcoming message of celebration.

The beautiful weather in southern Europe and the smiling faces did little to cheer the archduke and the archduchess. Less than an hour earlier, the pair had narrowly escaped death when an assassin had hurled a bomb at their car. The archduke's driver had managed to deflect the bomb from the car, and the deadly missile had bounced off the back

Franz Ferdinand and his wife, Sophie, were greeted warmly when they visited Sarajevo.

of the automobile and exploded beneath the car. Pieces of the bomb had injured a number of people, including one in the archduke's party. The man was rushed to the hospital with pieces of the weapon lodged in the back of his head. Although the visiting royal couple had escaped with a few scratches, they were still shaken. Now they sat side by side as the car headed toward the city hall.

ANGER IN BOSNIA

In October 1908, Austria-Hungary upset people around the world by annexing the small Balkan province of Bosnia and Herzegovina. The move sparked anger and protest from many Bosnians. People in the neighboring nation of Serbia were also outraged. Serbians dreamed of a united Slavic nation that included Serbia, Bosnia and Herzegovina, and other nations in the Balkans.

After the attempted murders, Bosnia's military governor, General Oskar Potiorek, did little to ensure the royal couple's safety on the final day of their visit to Sarajevo. When the archduke's aides asked for soldiers to be stationed along the route, Potiorek refused. He scornfully asked the worried aides, "Do you think that Sarajevo is full of assassins?"

After the visit to the city hall, the archduke decided to visit those wounded in the earlier attack. To make the ride to the hospital safer, it was decided that a new route would be chosen. Instead of winding through the narrow streets of Sarajevo's Muslim Quarter, the motorcade would return the way it had come: The archduke and his wife would travel back along Sarajevo's broadest street, Appel Quay.

General Potiorek, riding with the Austrian royals as part of their group, forgot to tell the archduke's driver of this change in plans. When the driver turned down a narrow alley to head into the city's Muslim section, the general immediately yelled, "What is this? This is the wrong way!" He ordered the chauffeur to stop the car and turn around.

The order could not have come at a worse time. Just steps away from the archduke and his wife stood a 19-year-old Bosnian man named Gavrilo Princip. For weeks, he and his accomplices had planned an assassination of the Austrian archduke, whom many Bosnians despised. Now

The warm weather on June 28, 1914, made it possible for the archduke and his wife (back seat) to travel to Sarajevo's city hall in an open car.

standing just feet away from Franz Ferdinand, the teenager seized his chance to act. He stepped toward the archduke. Princip later remembered his next fateful actions: "I got hold of my handgun and aimed it at the car without really looking. I even looked away when I fired."

Princip quickly fired two shots. The first shot passed through the side of the car and struck the archduchess in the abdomen. The second shot found its intended target and directly hit Franz Ferdinand in the neck. The bullet severed his jugular vein and lodged in his spine. A thin stream

After firing the fatal shots, Gavrilo Princip (second from right) was quickly grabbed by bystanders and nearby police officers.

13

of blood spurted from the archduke's mouth, spattering Count Franz von Harrach, the man who was sitting near him in the car. The archduchess saw her husband's blood and cried out, "For God's sake, what has happened to you?" Then she slumped over and slid to the floor. She would die from her wound.

Harrach and General Potiorek were not worried about the archduchess. They believed that she had fainted from fright. Instead, the two turned their attention to the gravely injured archduke. However, Franz Ferdinand seemed to sense that his wife had not only fainted. He cried out, "Sopherl! Sopherl! Don't die! Live for my children."

THE MYSTERY OF A MISSING PISTOL

In 2004, a group of librarians in Austria discovered a number of unusual artifacts. After some research, they found that one of these items was the pistol Gavrilo Princip used to assassinate Archduke Franz Ferdinand and his wife. This gun—along with other assassination mementos—was stashed away at the home of Jesuit priests in southern Austria. Historians believe that after the assassination, Father Anton Puntigam was given Princip's gun by police for safekeeping. He had been a witness to the murder of the royal couple. Over the years, the priest became obsessed with gathering items relating to the assassination. Hoping to open a museum in the couple's honor, Puntigam kept the deadly pistol and managed to collect the unused bombs and pistols carried by the other would-be assassins.

As the archduke sagged to the side, Harrach grabbed his collar and held him upright. When asked if he was in pain, Franz Ferdinand said, "It is nothing, it is nothing."

The jacket worn by Franz Ferdinand at the time of his death was stained with his blood.

He then became unconscious. The royal couple was rushed to the governor's house, and doctors were called to treat them. But it was too late. Sophie died before doctors could arrive, and Franz Ferdinand lived only a short time longer. The heir to the throne of Austria-Hungary was dead, and the entire world was about to change. 🔖

A Fading Empire

Chapter

2

In 1848, an 18-year-old Habsburg royal named Franz Josef became the ruler of Austria. The young man took control of an aging empire that was declining in power. Early in his reign, Franz Josef involved Austria in a number of unsuccessful conflicts that strained the empire's relations with France, Russia, and Germany. In the first 20 years of his reign, Austria lost its territories in Italy and Germany. In 1867, he managed to preserve the rest of his empire by allowing Hungary to become a separate and self-governing state within the new Austro-Hungarian empire. Although Hungary had its own government and political leader, Franz Josef remained its king.

As the 20th century neared, Austria-Hungary was an empire made up of 17 provinces.

Franz Josef I ruled Austria and its territories for nearly 70 years.

Each province had its own culture, ethnic groups, languages, and customs. Many of the provinces resented being controlled by a foreign power. The spirit of nationalism, a belief that countries and groups of people have the right to govern themselves, grew stronger within Austria-Hungary. By the late 1800s, a crisis within the empire seemed unavoidable.

Throughout the 1800s, nationalism had become an important political force in different regions of the world. As the movement gained strength, people in Austria-Hungary, Germany, Italy, and other regions formed groups such as political parties, patriotic societies, and student clubs to further their nationalist goals. They wrote poetry, published books and news-papers, and flew flags to inspire others to join their causes. Only a very

THE HABSBURGS

Austria-Hungary had its roots in the Habsburg Empire, which was a powerful dynasty founded in the late 1200s by a German prince named Rudolf. In 1273, Rudolf was made ruler of the Holy Roman Empire, a monarchy that included parts of Italy, Germany, and Austria. For the next 600 years, the Habsburgs dominated central Europe, ruling the region with an iron fist. Between the 1200s and the early 1900s, the Habsburgs at one time controlled Germany, Austria, Hungary, Croatia, Spain, Portugal, Bohemia (now part of the Czech Republic), Galicia and Lodomeria (now part of Poland and Ukraine), Transylvania (present-day western Romania), and Tuscany (a region in Italy). Their influence also extended beyond Europe: In 1864, Archduke Ferdinand Maximilian, brother of Franz Josef, took the throne as emperor of Mexico.

Austria-Hungary, 1914

GERMANY

Wroclaw

RUSSIA

Prague

L'viv

AUSTRIA

Munich

Vienna ⊗

Bratislava

⊗ Budapest

LIECHTENSTEIN

SWITZERLAND

A U S T R I A - H U N G A R Y

Lake Balaton

HUNGARY

Trieste

Zagreb

Croatia

ROMANIA

ITALY

Bucharest ⊗

Bosnia

Belgrade ⊗

Sarajevo

SAN MARINO

Adriatic Sea

SERBIA

BULGARIA

MONTENEGRO

Sofia ⊗

Cetinje ⊗

ALBANIA

Austria		Hungary	
Bosnia		Croatia	

0   100   200 mi.
0   100   200 km

few of the groups—such as the Fenian Society in Ireland—turned to violence and terrorism as a way of making changes.

The man who stood to inherit the problems of the ailing empire in the early 1900s was Franz Ferdinand Erzherzog Von Osterreich-este, a nephew of Emperor Franz Josef. Franz Ferdinand was born December 18, 1863, in Graz, Austria, to Archduke Karl Ludwig and his wife, Maria Annunciata. Franz Ferdinand's mother died when he was young, and the boy was raised by his stepmother, Maria Theresia of Braganza.

In the early 1900s, Austria-Hungary was one of the largest and most powerful empires in the world.

19

Franz Ferdinand and his two younger brothers, Otto and Ferdinand Karl, were constantly on the move between castles and hunting lodges. The boys had private tutors to educate them and were also taught to hunt, dance, and ride horses. Like their father, the three boys bore the title of archduke, used by Habsburg royals for centuries. Archdukes were the same as princes in other royal houses.

Franz Ferdinand (left) and his younger brother Otto were the oldest of Karl Ludwig's six children.

After his schooling was finished, Franz Ferdinand chose a military path. The young man took to soldiering and rose quickly in the ranks. At the age of 21 he was made a captain, and over the next two decades, he rose to the rank of general.

Those who met the archduke were often frightened of him. A large man with icy blue eyes and a thick, black mustache, Franz Ferdinand was not thought of as kind. He once said, "When I meet anyone for the first time, I assume he is good for nothing and only gradually change my opinion if he proves otherwise."

The archduke had a short temper and often acted hostile toward those around him. One man who worked for Franz Ferdinand remembered what the archduke was like:

> *Ministers and other high officials rarely waited on the Archduke without beating hearts. He was capable of flying out at people and terrifying them to such a degree that they lost their heads.*

Another man told a story of the angry archduke using his sword to hack at the cushions on his train. As a result of his personality, Franz Ferdinand was not a beloved figure to the Austrian people.

HUNTING

One of Franz Ferdinand's favorite pastimes was hunting. The archduke was an expert marksman and could even shoot holes in coins tossed into the air. On train trips, he sometimes opened the window and shot game while traveling. He was known to kill hundreds of pheasants and hares at a time. Just four years before his death, he killed his 5,000th stag.

For the first 26 years of his life, Franz Ferdinand was not the heir to the Austro-Hungarian throne. That honor rested with Archduke and Crown Prince Rudolf, the only son of Emperor Franz Josef. On January 30, 1889, however, Rudolf killed

Crown Prince Rudolf dressed in Hungarian clothing to pose for a photograph.

his young mistress and himself at Mayerling, a hunting lodge near Vienna. Because the crown prince had no male children, Franz Ferdinand's father became the next in line to the throne. Seven years later, when Karl Ludwig died of typhoid, a disease that affects the intestines, Franz Ferdinand became heir to the empire.

Franz Ferdinand's relationship with his uncle—never a warm one—became even worse after Rudolf's death. The archduke was excluded from any role in governing the empire. He also sensed the emperor's dislike for him. "I seem to be regarded as though I am to blame for the stupidity of Mayerling," he wrote. "Formerly I was not treated so coldly; it seems the sight of me evokes painful memories."

THE MYSTERY OF MAYERLING

The death of Crown Prince Rudolf has posed a mystery for more than 100 years. At first, the royal family reported that the heir to the throne had died of an epileptic seizure or of heart problems. No mention was made of the death of his 17-year-old mistress, Baroness Maria Vetsera. Later it was reported that the two had carried out a suicide pact. Other people theorized that the prince's liberal beliefs had led to his murder, with Vetsera being in the wrong place at the wrong time. Historians now believe that the 30-year-old heir to the throne suffered from a mental illness, probably depression. His frustration with his father and his unhappy marriage may have led him to his last desperate act: He shot Vetsera, and then hours later turned the gun on himself.

In the years after Rudolf's death, Franz Ferdinand became preoccupied with his personal life. In about 1894, he began spending time with the three unmarried daughters of Archduke Friedrich and Archduchess Isabella, members of the Habsburg family. During the coming years, many people— including Isabella—believed that Franz Ferdinand was courting the oldest daughter, Marie Christina. But eventually, the truth came to light: The archduke, now 35 years old, was wooing 31-year-old Sophie Chotek von Chotkova und Wognin, a lady-in-waiting to the Archduchess Isabella.

A huge scandal resulted from the discovery. Sophie, only a minor noble, was considered a commoner by the Habsburgs. As such, she could never marry into the Habsburg family. The emperor demanded that Franz Ferdinand give up this unsuitable relationship.

Franz Ferdinand, for once defying his powerful uncle, refused to give up Sophie. He sent a pleading letter to his uncle:

> *I have once again summoned up courage to approach Your Majesty. Last time Your Majesty told me you thought that my marriage could harm the Monarchy. I venture most humbly to say that this marriage, because it will make me happy and give me strength to bear my responsibilities, will enable me to do my duty to the Monarchy far better than if I have to spend the rest of my life consumed with unfulfilled longing, unhappy, lonely.*

He later told the Austrian prime minister that marrying Sophie was a question of "my life, my existence, and my future."

24

Although Franz Josef did not respond to the letter, he finally agreed to allow the marriage—

but only after reading letters in favor of the union from Pope Leo XIII, Kaiser Wilhelm of Germany, and Tsar Nicholas of Russia. The emperor insisted that the archduke and his bride agree to certain conditions. For example, Sophie could never become the empress of Austria, and

Emperor Franz Josef (left) and his nephew Franz Ferdinand rode side by side at a military exercise in Hungary.

their children would never succeed to the throne of Austria-Hungary.

In addition, Sophie had to follow strict rules laid out by the royal court. She couldn't ride in a carriage next to her husband. She couldn't sit in the royal box with him when they went to the opera. And she ranked below all the other archduchesses and was forced to stand behind them in line and sit below them at formal dinners. Even after death, she would be treated as an inferior: Sophie was banned from being buried in the royal Habsburg crypt.

On July 1, 1900, Franz Ferdinand and Sophie finally wed. Emperor Franz Josef, still angry that his nephew had placed his personal life before his duty to the empire, refused to attend the ceremony. However, he did send a telegram giving Sophie the title "Princess von Hohenberg." Years later, the emperor would raise her to the title of duchess, allowing her the right to be addressed as "Highness."

Franz Ferdinand's marriage to Sophie was a happy one. In the coming years, the pair had three children: Sophie in 1901, Maximilian in 1902, and Ernst in 1904. After the birth of Ernst, Franz Ferdinand wrote to his stepmother:

> *You don't know how happy I am with my family, and how I can't thank God enough for all my happiness. The most intelligent thing I've ever done in my life has been the marriage*

> *to my Soph. And our children. They are my whole delight and pride. I sit with them and admire them the whole day because I love them so.*

The royal couple avoided the Austrian court from which the empire ruled in Vienna, choosing a quieter life at home with their children. They did so in part because of the strict rules that highlighted Sophie's lower social standing. Only in foreign courts and countries was the archduchess treated with the respect and honor her husband felt she deserved. So when the two were invited to visit Sarajevo in June 1914, the chance to sit side by side with his wife may have enticed Franz Ferdinand to agree to a trip into such an unsafe region.

Troubled Region

In the early 1900s, anti-Austrian sentiment in parts of the Austro-Hungarian empire had reached an all-time high. The most troubled region in Austria-Hungary was the empire's Balkan territories. These territories were located on the Balkan Peninsula in southeast Europe, to the south of Austria. In 1900, the present-day Balkan nations of Croatia, Slovenia, and Bosnia and Herzegovina were all part of the empire.

Austria-Hungary was not the first empire to control part of the Balkans. During its long and troubled history, the region was conquered by the Romans, the Slavs, and finally the Turkish Ottoman Empire in the late 1300s. For hundreds of years, the Turks controlled the Balkan region. They brought the Muslim religion and Turkish architecture and customs to the Balkans.

Minarets on Muslim places of worship could be seen all around Sarajevo in the early 1900s.

Throughout the 1800s, the Balkan countries of Montenegro, Serbia, Romania, and Bulgaria and neighboring Greece all gained independence from the Ottoman Empire. In 1878, the Ottoman Turks were driven out of the Balkans by Russia during the Russo-Turkish War. With the Ottomans no longer firmly in control, some of its territories in the region were divided up among Austria, Russia, and Great Britain. Under the Treaty of Berlin, Austria won the right to temporarily govern Bosnia and Herzegovina. The Ottomans retained a grip on only a few areas in the southern part of the peninsula.

Serbia, a neighboring country to Bosnia and Herzegovina, was unhappy with the new treaty. Many Serbian people dreamed of uniting the entire region in one large Slavic nation known as Yugoslavia, "Land of the South Slavs." Such a nation would include Bosnia and Herzegovina, Slovenia, Croatia, Montenegro, and parts of Macedonia. Serbia would be the center of this large nation, and a common language would unite the country.

Not everyone in Bosnia and Herzegovina supported Serbia's goal of creating Yugoslavia, or "Greater Serbia," as the proposed nation was sometimes known. The country was home not only to Serbs but also to Croats and Bosnian Muslims who had adopted the Islamic religion. The groups maintained their unique identities and soon formed their own competing political parties, each with different goals. Bosnian Muslims, for example, wanted to remain separate from their Slav neighbors.

Anti-Austrian feelings in the Balkans skyrocketed in 1908. In October, the empire annexed Bosnia and Herzegovina and took control of the province.

In 1908, many newspapers ran political cartoons that depicted the outrage many people felt when Austria-Hungary annexed Bosnia and Herzegovina.

31

Emperor Franz Josef worried that Bosnia might be moving toward independence. He told an aide, "If Bosnia becomes independent, we shall lose Croatia and Dalmatia. We can never agree to this, we have already lost enough territory."

Serbs in Bosnia and in Serbia were furious. People in Belgrade, Serbia's capital, held anti-Austria demonstrations, and Serbia's government began to prepare for war against the empire. A violent conflict was prevented only when Russia stepped in and warned the Serbians that they should calm down. Without the backing and support of its strongest ally, Serbia agreed.

Although Russia had helped prevent a war, the nation's leaders were not happy with Austria's annexation of Bosnia. Other European nations agreed that the emperor's latest move was in clear violation of the Treaty of Berlin. Archduke Franz Ferdinand spoke out against the annexation with the words, "In general I am absolutely opposed to all such dissipations of

THE TREATY OF BERLIN

In July 1878, representatives of the world's strongest nations signed a document intended to put an end to the Russo-Turkish War. The nations who attended were Austria-Hungary, France, Germany, Italy, the Ottoman Empire, Russia, Great Britain, and the United States. Under the terms of the Treaty of Berlin, as the document became known, the Ottoman Empire lost great chunks of its territory, including Romania, Bosnia and Herzegovina, Serbia, Montenegro, and Bulgaria. While some of the Slavic nations were given independence, Bosnia and Herzegovina was put under the administrative control of Austria-Hungary.

strength. I would prefer that no action be taken." As usual, his opinion was ignored. In the coming years, Bosnia would prove to be a troublesome and rebellious colony.

In the years following the annexation, other countries in the region fought for and won more freedoms and territory. During the Balkan Wars in 1912 and 1913, Greece, Serbia, Bulgaria, and Montenegro drove the Turks out of all Balkan lands. With these victories, Serbs in Bosnia began working to upset the balance of Austrian power in their country.

Greek soldiers were among the troops that drove the Turks out of the Balkans during the Balkan Wars.

33

Franz Ferdinand recognized that the empire was in danger of collapsing. One historian at this time called Austria-Hungary a "broken pot held together with a piece of wire."

Franz Ferdinand had opposed the annexation of Bosnia, but he now began creating plans that might hold the fragile empire together. He offered ideas to please the Slavic people. One idea was to create a tri-monarchy, an empire made up of Austria,

Franz Josef ruled Austria-Hungary until his death at the age of 86.

Hungary, and a Slavic nation. Like Hungary, the Slavs would have their own government and rule themselves. Others believed that the archduke was considering a federation made up of 16 states with equal rights.

Many Austrian and Hungarian officials—and Franz Josef himself—were upset when they learned of Franz Ferdinand's ideas. It was clear that Franz Ferdinand meant to give up the strong imperial powers that Franz Josef was trying so hard to keep. If a Slavic nation was formed, those who helped control Austria-Hungary would lose their powers, too. To keep control, Franz Josef's advisers were willing to risk a war. ◣

Planning
Revolution

A fter Bosnia and Herzegovina was annexed in 1908, several groups formed in Serbia to promote anti-Austrian sentiment. One of the largest and most successful was Narodna Odbrana, which means "the People's Defense" or "National Defense." This group, made up of Serbian politicians and military officers, formed just days after the annexation. The group trained people to spy on and fight against the Austrians in Bosnia. Later the group worked to spread Serbian culture and anti-Austrian propaganda in an attempt to influence public opinion.

As National Defense turned away from violence, a new group formed to continue the fight against Austrians in Bosnia. This group, founded in 1911, was called Ujedinjenje ili Smrt, or "Unification or Death." Most people, however,

Le Petit Journal

Le Petit Journal **5** CENTIMES SUPPLÉMENT ILLUSTRÉ **5** CENTIMES ABONNEMENTS

Le Petit Journal agricole, 5 cent. ~~ La Mode du Petit Journal, 10 cent.
Le Petit Journal illustré de la Jeunesse, 10 cent.

On s'abonne sans frais dans tous les bureaux de poste

DIMANCHE 18 OCTOBRE 1908 Numéro 935

An illustration in a Paris-based newspaper depicted Bosnia and Herzegovina being torn away.

knew it by its popular name: Crna Ruka, or the "Black Hand." One of the leading forces behind the Black Hand was Dragutin Dimitrijevic, a Serbian army officer and head of the intelligence section of the Serbian army's general staff.

The Black Hand was made up mostly of Serbian army officers but also included Serbian government officials, lawyers, professors, and journalists. It was headquartered in Belgrade and often operated hand in hand with the Serbian government. For example, the government appointed Black Hand members to important posts at border stations near Austria. In return, government officials were often given information about Black Hand plans in advance.

Black Hand leader Dragutin Dimitrijevic was considered a hero by many Serbians.

The Black Hand's goal was to drive those it called Austrian oppressors out of Bosnia and the Balkans. Its charter read:

> *This organization was created in order to realize the national ideal, the unification of all Serbs. This organization prefers terrorist action to cultural activities; it will therefore remain secret.*

Within three years of its founding, the Black Hand had grown to include as many as 2,500 members. A small central committee made up of 10 key members headed the group. Like today's terrorist organizations, the Black Hand also had many smaller cells that knew little about other cells or the group leaders. If one cell was discovered, it could not jeopardize the work of the others.

Dragutin Dimitrijevic, whose code name was Apis, the Latin word for "bee," had masterminded a successful plot to assassinate King Alexander and Queen Draga of Serbia in 1903. The attack left Dimitrijevic seriously wounded but revered by Serb nationalists. After he recovered, he was celebrated by Serbia's parliament as the "savior of the fatherland."

One of the Black Hand's chief methods of attack against its enemies was to encourage and train young Serbs to carry out political assassinations. To accomplish this, the Black Hand sponsored training camps and schools for would-be terrorists. At the camps, young men learned how to throw bombs, shoot firearms, and become effective spies for the Slavic unity movement.

At this time, young, idealistic nationalists in Belgrade often met in the city's coffeehouses, where they could openly discuss their hatred for Austria and their desire for a Slavic state. One young man who visited Belgrade's coffeehouses was Gavrilo Princip, a teenager from Bosnia. Princip was born in 1894 to poor peasants in Obljaj, a small village in Bosnia and Herzegovina. Life was hard for the Princip family. Like other peasants

THE OATH OF THE BLACK HAND

Those who wanted to join the Black Hand were asked to take a solemn oath: "I swear by the Sun that warms me, by the earth that nourishes me, before God, by the blood of my ancestors, on my honor and on my life, that I will from this moment till my death be faithful to the laws of this organization, and I will always be ready to make any sacrifice for it. I swear that I will take all the secrets of the organization with me into my grave. May God confound me and my comrades in this organization judge me if I trespass against or either consciously or unconsciously fail to keep this oath!"

39

in the village, Princip, his parents, and his two siblings lived in a small one-room hut with no windows. The only sunlight to enter the home came through a small hole cut in the roof to let out smoke from a cooking fire.

When Princip was 13, he was offered a scholarship to a school in Sarajevo. There he met other students who felt resentment and hatred for the Austrians,

ASSASSINATION AS A POLITICAL WEAPON

The late 1800s and early 1900s was a bloody time to be a ruler or a political leader. Beginning in 1881, dozens of important leaders, royalty, and minor officials were murdered. Many of the assassinations were carried out by members of small terrorist groups, people who wanted to disrupt or overthrow their states' governments. By choosing royal or important targets, the assassins drew international attention to their causes and beliefs. The assassinated included:

- Tsar Alexander II, Russia (1881)
- President James Garfield, United States (1881)
- President Marie Francois Sadi Carnot, France (1894)
- Prime Minister Antonio Canovas, Spain (1897)
- Empress Elizabeth, Austria-Hungary (1898)
- King Humbert I, Italy (1900)
- President William McKinley, United States (1901)
- King Alexander and Queen Draga, Serbia (1903)
- Grand Duke Sergei, Russia (1905)
- King Carlos, Portugal (1908)
- Prince Hirobumi Ito, Japan (1909)
- Prime Minister Petr Stolypin, Russia (1911)
- King George, Greece (1913)

the "vampires and oppressors," as the local newspapers called them. The young students read radical literature and spoke of somehow striking a blow against these hated occupiers.

The assassination of U.S. President James Garfield on July 2, 1881, was one of many political murders.

In 1912, Princip and 19 other boys were expelled from high school for taking part in a violent demonstration. Princip traveled to Belgrade to finish his education. In Belgrade, he volunteered to serve in the Serb army, but he was turned away for being physically unfit to fight. He then returned to Bosnia.

In early 1914, Princip went back to Belgrade. He and his friends again talked of striking a blow for a Slavic state. But Princip was more serious than before and had come to believe that the only way to gain attention for the Slavic cause was to

As a young man, Gavrilo Princip learned to despise the Austrians who controlled his native country.

assassinate an important figure from Austria-Hungary. He decided to target a member of the royal family or a high-ranking diplomat.

Some historians believe that Dimitrijevic encouraged Princip to choose Franz Ferdinand as a target. After the assassination, however, the young assassins claimed that the idea to target the archduke was Princip's alone. Princip said that he came up with the idea in late March, after reading of Franz Ferdinand's upcoming visit to Sarajevo.

Princip enlisted three of his closest friends to help him carry out the plot. The first was Nedeljko Cabrinovic, a 20-year-old high school dropout from Bosnia who was working at a state printing house in Belgrade. The second was Trifko Grabez, the 19-year-old son of an orthodox priest in Bosnia. Princip and Grabez had met while attending school in Belgrade.

The third friend brought into the plan was Danilo Ilic, 24, a Bosnian who had served as a stretcher-bearer during the Balkan Wars. Ilic was also the leader of Sarajevo's Mlada Bosna, or "Young Bosnia" group, which may have had ties to the Black Hand in Serbia. Princip wrote to Ilic in Sarajevo, informing him of the plot and asking him to find other Bosnians to help with the assassination. Unlike the other assassins, however, Ilic would not carry any weapons. He would serve as an organizer and a go-between.

SARAJEVO, BOSNIA'S CAPITAL

Sarajevo became an important trade and cultural center in the late 1400s, after Turks invaded and took control of the region. As part of the Muslim Ottoman Empire, the city grew and flourished. It became famous for its many mosques and for craftspeople who wove beautiful, intricate carpets. In 1878, when Austria-Hungary took over from the Turks, Sarajevo was named Bosnia and Herzegovina's political center. It also became the heart of Bosnian resistance to Austrian rule.

The assassins were also given packets of cyanide, a type of poison. After the assassination, the men were to kill themselves by taking the cyanide. This would prevent them from being captured and telling police where they got their weapons.

In late May, Princip and his two friends began the journey from Belgrade to Sarajevo. The Black Hand assisted them on the way there. The group's network of members helped the assassins get

43

cheaper train fares and pass through customs and provided them with places to stay. Many of these people would later be tried for their small roles in the crime.

Some historians believe that the government of Serbia had advance warning that assassins were heading to Sarajevo to kill the archduke. Because of the government's close ties to the Black Hand, Prime Minister Nikola Pasic may have learned of the plot in May. Some historians think that Pasic ordered the three Bosnian youths arrested before they left Serbia. By the time the order was issued, however, the young men were gone.

Although Danilo Ilic carried no weapons on the day of Franz Ferdinand's assassination, he was one of the key planners of the plot to murder the archduke.

Pasic had his ambassador to Austria-Hungary warn Austrian officials of a possible attempt on Franz Ferdinand's life. However, the ambassador did not speak of an actual plot. Instead he suggested that harm might come to the archduke during military exercises. He said:

> *Some young Serb might put a live rather than a blank cartridge in his gun, and fire it. That bullet might hit the man who provoked him. Therefore it might be good and reasonable if Archduke Franz Ferdinand were not to go to Sarajevo.*

Later many would point to the statement as evidence that Serbian officials knew about the assassination and did little to prevent it.

In Belgrade, Princip and his co-conspirators were put in contact with Major Vojin Tankosic, a key member of the Black Hand and Dimitrijevic's chief aide. It is believed that Tankosic assigned one of his men—Milan Ciganovic—to supply the young men with four revolvers and six small bombs. The bombs, rectangular in shape and weighing only 2½ pounds (1 kilogram) each, were small enough to be hidden inside a coat pocket. ◣

In Sarajevo

5

As Gavrilo Princip and his friends made their way to Sarajevo, Danilo Ilic was busy looking for others to take part in the assassination. He quickly tracked down three people. The first was Mehmed Mehmedbasic, a 27-year-old carpenter and the only Muslim in the group of assassins. Mehmedbasic told Ilic that he had planned to assassinate Bosnia's military governor, Oskar Potiorek, earlier in the year. He had lost his nerve, he said, when he saw the police. The other two were 17-year-old Vaso Cubrilovic and his 18-year-old friend, Cvetko Popovic. Cubrilovic had recently been expelled from high school for leaving class when the Habsburg anthem was played.

On June 4, 1914, Princip, Cabrinovic, and Grabez arrived in Sarajevo. Once there, they went their separate ways to enjoy what they believed to be their last days alive in their homeland. While his friends went to visit their families, Princip stayed with Ilic.

Gavrilo Princip (left) and Nedeljko Cabrinovic (right) met with Milan Ciganovic (center) before the assassination.

The same day in Vienna, Austria, the archduke's trip to Bosnia was officially announced. The purpose of the trip was to inspect the Bosnian army. During his visit, the archduke would watch several military exercises organized by General Potiorek. The trip was also intended to show the empire's good will toward Bosnia: A member of the Habsburg family had not visited the Balkan country since 1910.

Franz Ferdinand knew the dangers of traveling into the unsettled area. He understood that someone in his position was subject to the threat of assassination. He once said, "We are all constantly in danger of death. One must simply trust in God."

Still he chose to make the journey and to bring his wife, Sophie, with him. Some historians believe that the archduke brought Sophie to Bosnia because there, outside of Austria, she could be beside him. She could sit by his side at dinner and walk by his side during public ceremonies. Sophie wanted to make the trip. She believed that assassins would be less likely to attack her husband if she was at his side. And the trip would nearly coincide with the couple's 14th wedding anniversary.

Almost as soon as the trip was announced, however, Franz Ferdinand may have begun to have second thoughts. He told the emperor that his health was not good and that he might cancel the visit. After a minor scheduling change, Franz Ferdinand erupted:

> *Tell Colonel Bardolff that if he should spoil our taste for the Bosnian trip even more than he has done so by these daily difficulties and troubles, he can hold the maneuvers by himself. I won't go at all then.*

Despite Franz Ferdinand's misgivings, he and Sophie began the journey to Bosnia and Herzegovina on June 23, leaving their castle in Bohemia to travel by train to Vienna.

Franz Ferdinand kept photographs of his children on his desk at his castle in Bohemia.

49

Franz Ferdinand and Sophie planned to use the trip to Bosnia to celebrate their 14th wedding anniversary.

From the beginning of the journey, Archduke Franz Ferdinand seemed to have a premonition of what was to come. On the day he left, the archduke gave his personal assistant a gold watch and asked him to watch after Sophie and the children if anything happened to him on the trip. In addition, his special car caught on fire and could not be used. Franz Ferdinand said, "Well, that's a promising beginning for this trip."

In Vienna, the archduke and his wife parted ways. Sophie continued by train to Budapest in Hungary. As the train made its way into Bosnia, the archduchess was greeted at every station by flags flying and people waving in welcome. On the morning of June 25, she arrived at the Bosnian town of Ilidza where many people had turned out to welcome her despite the pouring rain. From there, she was taken to the Hotel Bosna, the resort where she and her husband would spend their time in Bosnia.

Franz Ferdinand took a different route to Bosnia. From Vienna, a special train was waiting to carry him to the shore of the Adriatic Sea. But the train car assigned to him had an electrical problem, and candles had to be lit. Franz Ferdinand's secretary remembered the archduke saying, "What do you think about these lights? Just like in a grave, isn't it?"

At the docks, Franz Ferdinand boarded an Austrian battleship and spent the next 18 hours crossing the Adriatic Sea. He was greeted at the mouth of the Narenta River in Bosnia by Potiorek. Together, the two boarded a smaller boat and headed up the river to catch a train to Ilidza. Along the way, Franz Ferdinand was welcomed

On June 25, Franz Ferdinand arrived at the train station in Ilidza, a small town near Sarajevo.

by people with flags and colorful rugs flying from their windows in greeting. When the people caught sight of the archduke, they waved and cheered. Men in native costumes shot guns into the air in celebration of the visit.

After both Franz Ferdinand and Sophie had arrived in Ilidza, they made the 12-mile (19.2-kilometer) trip into Sarajevo to shop. They were soon surrounded by Bosnians who wanted to greet and see the royal couple. One person who was attracted by the gathering crowds was Gavrilo Princip. He was close enough to touch the archduke but did not take any action. He wanted to wait until June 28, three days later, when the rest of his assassin friends would be in place.

During the royal couple's trip to Sarajevo, General Potiorek was placed in charge of their safety. The archduke's dislike of security made guarding him a challenge. For example, Franz Ferdinand would often try to evade his security guards. He was also quick to let strangers— even suspicious-looking ones—approach him and speak to him.

Franz Ferdinand spent the two days after his arrival in Bosnia watching the military exercises that had been scheduled for him. While he watched the men drill, his wife visited schools and orphanages in the area. The archduke was pleased

TURN-OF-THE-CENTURY SARAJEVO

At the turn of the century, Sarajevo was a city where European and Turkish cultures collided and combined. In 1892, a member of Austria's parliament toured Bosnia and wrote: "Perfectly charming: the general view of the town as beautiful as anything of the kind in Europe: Set in the center of a great bowl, it is surrounded by range upon range of mountains, the lower ones being wooded, the higher ones heath-clad. Everywhere one sees the new Sarajevo, with its European buildings and modern streets pushing through the bright confusion of the old Oriental city. Mosques with their minarets rising up on all sides give the characteristic decorative note."

53

Franz Ferdinand received a warm greeting from Bosnian officials and citizens.

with the military performances, and on the evening of June 27, he telegraphed the emperor:

> The state of the troops, their training and performance have been excellent and beyond all praise. Tomorrow I shall visit Sarajevo and leave in the evening.

54

The couple planned to travel to the city hall, where a reception in their honor had been scheduled.

Later that evening, Franz Ferdinand and Sophie attended a formal dinner with Sarajevo's wealthiest and most powerful residents. At the event, Sophie greeted a man who had warned her not to come to Sarajevo. She told him:

You were wrong after all. Everywhere we have gone here we have been greeted with so much friendliness—and by every last Serb too—with so much cordiality and unsimulated warmth, that we are very happy about it!

The trip to the city hall the following day would be the crowning achievement of a successful visit. Neither the archduke nor the archduchess worried about riding through the streets of Sarajevo in an open car. The people who had warned the royal couple of danger and violence had been wrong: Throughout their trip, the archduke and his wife had been greeted with warmth and friendliness. The people of Bosnia, eager to see and cheer for Franz Ferdinand and Sophie, had put the royal couple at ease. After just one more day in Bosnia, the pair would return safely home to their three children. ◣

Assassination Day

The morning of June 28, 1914, was warm and sunny, a welcome change from the miserable weather of the previous days. Just before 10 A.M., Franz Ferdinand and Sophie arrived in Sarajevo from Ilidza. They were greeted by Potiorek and climbed into a large, open car for the short trip to the city hall.

The archduke's motorcade included six cars. The car in front of the royal couple's vehicle led the way. In the second car, Franz Ferdinand and Sophie were accompanied by General Potiorek and Count Franz von Harrach, the owner of the car. Four other cars carrying minor officials and assistants followed in back.

As crowds had gathered along the archduke's intended route to Sarajevo's city hall, the six Bosnian assassins took their assigned places.

The slow-moving motorcade made the archduke and his wife easy targets for their assassins.

Each one had a weapon, and each one had received a position along Franz Ferdinand's intended route to the city hall. They had also been given vials of cyanide, a deadly poison, to take once the plot had been accomplished. With the plan in place, they waited for the royal couple.

At about 10:15 A.M., the archduke's procession turned onto the Appel Quay, where six armed assassins stood waiting. Crowds of people lined both sides of the street and jostled to get a look at the heir to the throne and his wife. Noticeably missing from the parade route were soldiers and police officers.

As the cars turned onto the Appel Quay, Danilo Ilic slipped behind the first assassin on the route, Mehmed Mehmedbasic. Ilic whispered words of encouragement before continuing along his way. But as the car carrying the target slowly rolled past, Mehmedbasic did nothing. The second assassin, Vaso Cubrilovic, also failed to act. He later said he didn't want to hit Sophie.

The third assassin was Nedeljko Cabrinovic. As the car carrying the royal couple pulled up alongside him, the young Bosnian stepped away from the crowd, took the bomb from his pocket, and struck the cap of the weapon against a nearby light post. This action prepared the bomb to be thrown. Then Cabrinovic took aim at the general's green-feathered helmet and launched the bomb.

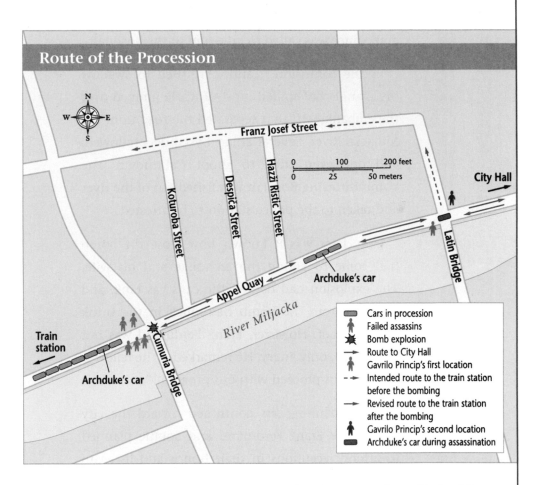

Route of the Procession

Franz Josef Street

City Hall

Koturoba Street

Despica Street

Hazži Ristic Street

| 0 | 100 | 200 feet |
| 0 | 25 | 50 meters |

Latin Bridge

Appel Quay

Archduke's car

River Miljacka

Train station

Ćumuria Bridge

Archduke's car

Cars in procession
Failed assassins
Bomb explosion
Route to City Hall
Gavrilo Princip's first location
Intended route to the train station before the bombing
Revised route to the train station after the bombing
Gavrilo Princip's second location
Archduke's car during assassination

As the bomb sailed through the air, the archduke's chauffeur caught a glimpse of it. He sped up, and the bomb bounced off the back of Franz Ferdinand's car and rolled underneath the car behind it. Seconds later, the bomb exploded. Cvetko Popovic, the fourth assassin, fled.

Although the bomb had missed its target, it had done some serious damage. Flying splinters injured a number of people. The most seriously wounded was one of Potiorek's aides, who had been hit in the back of the head by a bomb fragment. An

The Appel Quay was Sarajevo's main roadway and ran parallel to the Miljacka River.

59

ambulance was called to take him to the hospital.

In the confusion, Cabrinovic tried to swallow his cyanide but spilled most of it. He jumped over the embankment that separated the road from the Miljacka River. Several angry bystanders followed, and one even tried to shoot Cabrinovic. The bomb-throwing Bosnian was fished out of the river and taken to the police station to be arrested.

Only later was it known how close the bomb had come to killing the archduke and his wife. The explosion had dented the car's gas tank, and splinters from the bomb had stuck in the trunk and the roof. However, Franz Ferdinand was not frightened, only angry. He remarked, "The fellow is crazy. Let us proceed with our program."

The remaining cars continued toward the city hall. There Franz Ferdinand and Sophie planned to attend receptions in their honor and listen to speeches. Afterward they were to visit the National Museum and have lunch at the governor's home. Then they were to board the train once again and begin the trip back to Austria.

The procession moved along the same route, giving the last two assassins—Gavrilo Princip and Trifko Grabez—the chance to act. However, both of the men believed that the bomb attack had been a success. So when the archduke's vehicle rolled by, Princip was taken by surprise. Miserable at having missed his chance, he went to a nearby coffeehouse to consider his next move.

Grabez, the final assassin, did not act when the archduke's car passed him. He would later offer different reasons to explain his inaction. He stated that he was afraid of hurting women and children who were standing nearby and that he didn't want a friend who was with him to be blamed for his crime. Grabez went home and hid his weapons. Like most of the other conspirators, he was arrested within several days after Danilo Ilic supplied details of the assassination plot to authorities.

When the archduke and his wife stepped out of the car at city hall, word of the assassination attempt had not yet reached the lord mayor. He greeted the royal couple and launched into a speech he had prepared. The archduke quickly

Nedeljko Cabrinovic tried to escape arrest by jumping into the Miljacka River, but he was quickly caught.

61

interrupted the clueless official. Franz Ferdinand said, "What is the good of your speeches? I come to Sarajevo on a friendly visit and someone throws a bomb at me. This is outrageous."

Sophie calmed her husband, and the mayor was allowed to finish his welcome. Recovering, the

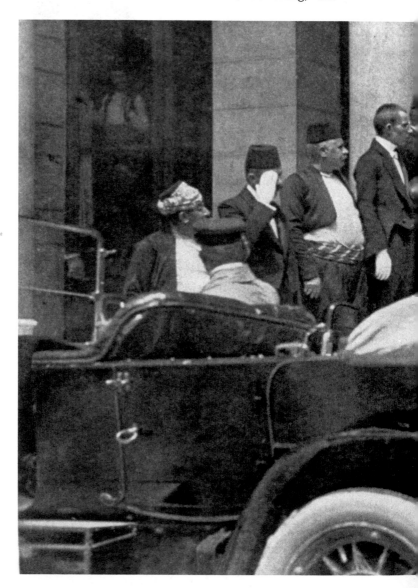

archduke responded in Serbo-Croatian:

> *May I ask you to give my cordial greetings to the inhabitants of this beautiful capital city, and assure you of my unchanged regard and favor.*

After the first assassination attempt, Franz Ferdinand continued his trip through Sarajevo.

Inside the city hall, a worried Franz Ferdinand tried to convince Sophie to go back to Vienna immediately while he visited the injured aide at the hospital and finished the rest of the official visit. Sophie, however, refused. She said, "As long as the archduke shows himself in public today, I will not leave him."

A newspaper illustration depicted the moment when Princip fired his gun at the royal couple.

The archduke's aides asked him to change his plans and remain inside the city hall until more

soldiers could be brought in to protect him. The archduke refused. Finally, the plan was made to return along the Appel Quay. At 10:45 A.M., the royal couple returned to their car and began the trip to the hospital. Count Harrach stood on the car's running board next to the archduke to shield the heir from any more assassination attempts.

Princip, meanwhile, had returned to his assigned spot, the same location where he had spent the morning waiting for Franz Ferdinand to pass by. When the archduke's car stopped just feet away from him, he couldn't believe his luck. Although the car was too close for Princip to use his bomb, he had another weapon at hand. He drew his pistol, stepped forward, and fired the fatal shots. Then he tried to shoot himself, but people standing near him grabbed his arm.

While the crowd beat the young assassin, Princip somehow managed to swallow the cyanide he had been given. However, the poison did not do its job. It merely made Princip sick and more miserable. Police finally managed to pull the angry mob off the assassin, rescuing him from almost certain death at their hands. He was taken into custody and brought to police headquarters. ◣

Grief and Consequences

The assassination of Franz Ferdinand and Sophie touched off riots in Sarajevo. The day after the killings, mobs of angry Muslims and Croats rioted against Serbs. Innocent people of Serbian descent became the targets of their anger. Schools, stores, and the offices of two Serb newspapers were destroyed. Bosnia's parliament condemned the killings and the violence.

In other parts of the world, the reaction to the archduke's death was more muted. This mild response was partly because Franz Ferdinand had been unloved by most people who knew him and partly because his marriage to a lady-in-waiting had alienated many of his powerful relatives. Unlike his dead cousin, Crown Prince Rudolf, Franz Ferdinand had not been a popular public figure.

After the assassination, mobs of Muslims and Croats attacked Serbs and their property throughout Sarajevo.

One U.S. official in Turkey reported on the general reaction to the deaths:

> On June 29th we heard of the assassination of the Grand Duke of Austria and his consort (wife). Everybody received the news calmly; there was, indeed, a stunned feeling that something momentous had happened, but there was practically no excitement.

Before they were shipped back to Austria, the bodies of Franz Ferdinand and his wife lay in state in Sarajevo.

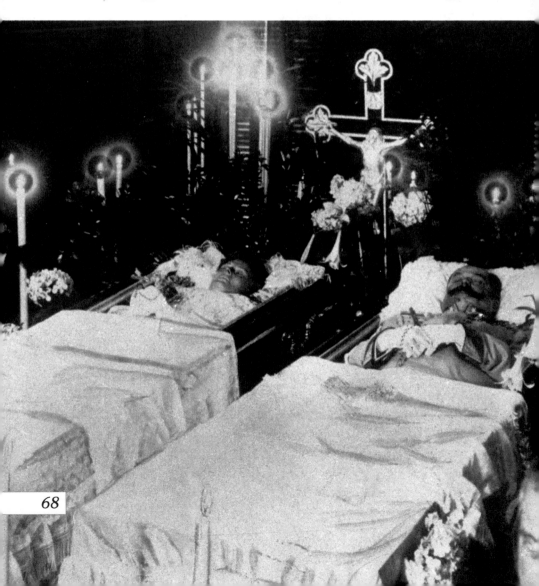

The bodies of the archduke and the archduchess were put on a train for the first leg of the journey back to Austria. In Vienna, royal officials made funeral arrangements. They requested that no foreign dignitaries or royals attend the funeral. The official excuse was that Emperor Franz Josef was far too weak and grief-stricken to receive them.

On July 3, 1914, the funeral for the pair took place at Hofburg Chapel in Vienna. To signify her inferior status, Sophie's coffin was placed inches below her husband's. The only flowers decorating the coffins were the white roses from their children—13-year-old Sophie, 11-year-old Max, and 10-year-old Ernst. Because of Sophie's presence in the church, her husband's coffin had no military or royal emblems placed upon it.

After the short ceremony, the coffins were taken by train to the family's home at Artstetten Castle. Although court rules had called for Franz Ferdinand to be buried in the royal crypt in Vienna, the archduke had left specific instructions that he was to be buried at Artstetten, side by side with his beloved wife. His final wish was respected.

COULD A FUNERAL HAVE PREVENTED WAR?

Modern historians believe that the decision not to invite important officials from other countries to Archduke Franz Ferdinand's funeral might have been one factor that led to World War I. If heads of state from nations such as Germany, Russia, France, Great Britain, and Serbia had attended the funeral, they might have been able to meet with Emperor Franz Josef and find ways to smooth out the upcoming crisis. Instead, the emperor was surrounded by Austrians and Hungarians who were hungry for war with Serbia.

After the deaths, the Serbian government acted quickly to make sure that the nation wasn't blamed for what had happened. Prime Minister Pasic ordered the coffeehouses and theaters closed and forbade public concerts and dances. He didn't want his people to be seen celebrating the murder of the heir to the Austro-Hungarian throne. In addition, the government newspaper condemned the actions.

It made no difference. Emperor Franz Josef and others in the Austro-Hungarian government were determined to use the killings as an excuse to settle an old score with Serbia. Soon after the funerals, the emperor sent Foreign Office Chief Alexander Hoyos to Germany with a letter for the kaiser, or German emperor:

THE ROYAL CHILDREN

After the deaths of their parents, the three royal children—Sophie, Maximilian, and Ernst—went to live with relatives in Bohemia (current-day Czech Republic). Four years later, the two boys were exiled from Bohemia, and all of their property and goods were confiscated. They then moved to Vienna, Austria. Sophie, allowed to remain in Bohemia with her aunt, married two years later and began raising a family. World War II brought even more misfortune to the family. In 1938, the two brothers were arrested by the Nazis and sent to Dachau, a concentration camp in Germany. The pair spent seven years imprisoned by Adolf Hitler's regime. They were finally released in 1945. Ernst died in 1954. His older brother, Maximilian, died eight years later. Although Sophie was not imprisoned during the war, two of her three sons died—one in battle, the other in a Soviet camp. At the end of the war, Sophie and her husband were forced to leave Czechoslovakia. She died in 1990.

[The assassination] is not the deed of a single individual, but the result of a well organized plot whose threads lead back to Belgrade. After the recent terrible events in Bosnia you too will be convinced that there is no longer any prospect of bridging the gulf between us and Serbia, and that the peaceful policy of all European monarchs will be threatened so long as this criminal agitation in Belgrade remains unpunished.

The lives of the three royal children—Sophie (left), Ernst (front left), and Maximilian— changed dramatically after the deaths of their parents.

71

After meeting with Hoyos, Kaiser Wilhelm II of Germany gave Austria-Hungary a promise of unconditional support if the nation went to war with Serbia. By giving this promise of German support, the kaiser hoped to scare Russia out of

Kaiser Wilhelm II of Germany gave his full support to Austria-Hungary.

interfering in any future Austrian-Serbian conflict. The promise, telegraphed to Franz Josef, read:

> *Finally, as far as concerns Serbia, His Majesty, of course, cannot interfere in the dispute now going on between Austria-Hungary and that country, as it is a matter not within his competence. The Emperor Franz Josef may, however, rest assured that His Majesty will faithfully stand by Austria-Hungary, as is required by the obligations of his alliance and of his ancient friendship.*

To satisfy the few officials in Austria-Hungary who still wanted to keep the peace, the emperor sent an ultimatum to Serbia. It arrived in Belgrade on July 23 and was written so Serbia could not possibly agree to all the terms. The notes from an Austrian council for war read:

> *All present, excepting the Hungarian Premier, hold that a purely diplomatic success, even if ending in a startling humiliation for Serbia, would be without value, and that, therefore, the demands to be put to Serbia must be so far-reaching as to pre-suppose a refusal, so that the way would be prepared for a radical solution by means of military intervention.*

When Serbian officials refused to accept the ultimatum, the Austro-Hungarian empire would have the excuse it needed to declare war.

On July 23, Count Berchtold, one of those who had pressured Emperor Franz Josef into agreeing to war, presented the ultimatum to Serbian officials. He gave them exactly 48 hours to respond. Serbian officials agreed to eight of the 10 demands:

- Suppress anti-Austrian publications.

- Disolve the National Defense and any other anti-Austrian groups.

- Fire anti-Austrian teachers.

- Fire anti-Austrian officers in the police and the military.

- Arrest two specific people, who had been implicated in the assassinations.

- Catch and prosecute all those who had any role in the assassinations.

- Explain why important Serbian officials were speaking in "hostile terms" about Austria-Hungary.

- Notify the Austro-Hungarian governments immediately when all the conditions were executed.

But they could not accept two demands. One of them would have allowed Austrian police to track down "subversives," or people who wanted to undermine Austria, in Serbia itself. The other would have allowed Austrian judges to come to Serbia to try these subversives. These two conditions violated the Serbian constitution.

Before responding, Serbia contacted Russia, its traditional ally. The tsar promised Serbian officials that Russian troops would defend them in case of war. And so, on July 25, just moments before

THE WILLY-NICKY LETTERS

Between July 29 and August 1, 1914, cousins Kaiser Wilhelm of Germany and Tsar Nicholas of Russia exchanged a series of telegrams. Today these telegrams are known as the Willy-Nicky Letters. The first, from Nicholas to Wilhelm, contained the following plea: "In this serious moment, I appeal to you to help me. An ignoble war has been declared to a weak country. ... I foresee that very soon I shall be overwhelmed by the pressure forced upon me and be forced to take extreme measures which will lead to war. I beg you in the name of our old friendship to do what you can to stop your allies from going too far." However, neither side would back down. The final telegram, sent by Kaiser Wilhelm on August 1, notified his cousin that he had mobilized his troops against Russia.

the 48-hour deadline expired, Prime Minister Pasic replied that Serbia could not possibly accept two of the terms of the ultimatum. War was now certain.

On July 28, exactly one month after the assassinations of Franz Ferdinand and Sophie, Austria-Hungary declared war against Serbia. The declaration of war consisted of two sentences:

> *The Royal Serbian Government not having answered in a satisfactory manner the note of July 23, 1914, the Imperial and Royal Government are themselves compelled to see to the safeguarding of their rights and interests, and, with this object, to have recourse to force of arms. Austria-Hungary consequently considers herself henceforward in state of war with Serbia.*

75

The conflict between Austria-Hungary and Serbia quickly grew into the first global war that the world had ever experienced. One after another, nations around the world became involved in the conflict, many bound by treaty to help nations that had chosen war. The first nation to enter the fray was Russia, bound by treaty to defend Serbia. On July 30, Tsar Nicholas mobilized his forces along Russia's border with both Austria-Hungary and Germany.

On August 1, Germany declared war against Russia. Two days later, Germany declared war on France, a nation bound by treaty to aid Russia. When neutral Belgium refused to allow German troops to enter on the way to France, Germany declared war on that country, too. Then Great Britain entered the war because of a pledge to defend Belgium. Britain's entry into the war committed all of its self-governing territories—including Australia and Canada—to the war as well.

By the end of summer, the Austro-Hungarian war against Serbia had grown into World War I. The conflict eventually pitted the Central Powers (Austria-Hungary, Germany, and the Ottoman Empire) against the Allies (Italy, France, Russia, Great Britain, Japan, and the United States).

Even before Franz Ferdinand's assassination, tensions among the major European powers had been running high. But instead of choosing diplomacy and a peaceful settlement to the problems of the Balkans, political and military leaders of the various nations deliberately chose war. Austria-Hungary was trying to keep its empire intact. German leaders were driven by strong nationalist feelings and a desire to expand their empire.

On August 4, 1914, a French newspaper announced that Germany had declared war against France.

World War I resulted in the destruction of many towns and cities throughout Europe, as well as the deaths of millions of people.

The Germans also believed they were surrounded by enemies, especially France and Russia. To prevent their own destruction, German leaders decided to act first. They may not have believed that the war would grow into a global conflict, but it did. With few international leaders choosing negotiation over bloodshed, World War I erupted into a deadly conflict.

By 1916, Emperor Franz Josef realized that the war he had helped to start was going to end badly for Austria-Hungary. Before his death in November, the emperor foresaw the breakup of his empire, something he had worked so hard to avoid. After his death, his grandnephew Karl I became the last Austro-Hungarian emperor. He reigned until the end of the war in 1918, when the empire was dissolved and the ancient Habsburg dynasty was no more. ◣

THE DEADLIEST CONFLICT

World War I became the deadliest conflict the world had known. During the course of the war, about 8.5 million soldiers were killed. As many as 13 million civilians also died during the war, many from disease or starvation. Russia, Germany, France, and Austria-Hungary suffered the greatest numbers of military casualties (deaths or injuries). These four nations accounted for seven out of every 10 casualties. The high death toll was caused, in part, by new weapons technology. Instead of bayonets, soldiers used machine guns, poison gas, and bombs to kill their enemies.

Justice for the Assassins

O n the same day in 1914 that Kaiser Wilhelm promised to aid Austria-Hungary, the last of the six assassins to be caught was taken into police custody. The only assassin who got away was Mehmed Mehmedbasic, who fled first to Montenegro and then to Serbia. Hundreds of people suspected of helping the assassins were arrested and questioned after June 28, but only 25 were charged with crimes.

The trials of Gavrilo Princip and the others began in Sarajevo on October 12. Eleven of those charged were under the age of 20. Eight people—including Princip and the other five main plotters—had been charged with treason, a crime punishable by death.

During the trial, all of the assassins admitted to being guilty of murder—except for Princip.

When asked if he was guilty, he said, "I am not a criminal, for I have removed an evildoer. I meant to do a good deed." He said he had not meant to kill the archduchess. Instead, he had hoped to kill Potiorek.

At the trial, all of the defendants agreed that they were guilty—except Gavrilo Princip (center).

Princip showed little emotion during the trial. One exception came when the testimony of Count Harrach was read out loud to the court. As Princip heard the last words of Sophie and Franz Ferdinand, he covered his eyes. When asked later if the account had made any impression upon him, he cried out, "Do you think I am an animal and have no feelings?"

Throughout the trial, the plotters continued to insist that Serbia and the Black Hand had nothing to do with the crime. Said Princip:

> *If it is asserted that somebody talked us into committing the assassination I can only say that this is not true. The idea of it was born in our hearts and we realized it.*

On October 23, at the end of the trial, the judge asked the 25 plotters to stand up if they were sorry for what they had done. Nearly all of them stood. Cabrinovic said that the last words of Franz Ferdinand had deeply affected him. He said, "We have profound regrets ... we did not know that the late Franz Ferdinand was a father." He asked the three orphaned children to forgive him. And he finished by saying, with tears in his eyes:

> *We are not criminals. We are honest people, animated by noble sentiments; we are idealists; we wanted to do good; we have loved our people; and we shall die for our ideals.*

One who did not stand was Princip. When the judge asked him to explain, he said that he was sorry for killing the archduchess and for leaving their children orphaned. He still remained unrepentant for killing the archduke.

On October 29, 1914, five of the six assassins on trial were found guilty of treason and murder. Because Bosnian law prevented people under the age of 20 from being executed for crimes, Princip, Grabez, and Cabrinovic were all sentenced to 20 years in prison, the maximum sentence. The judge also ordered that every June 28, on the anniversary of the assassination, Gavrilo Princip remain in a dark cell with no food and no mattress to lie on.

A STUDENT'S MOTIVES

During the trial, Cvetko Popovic explained his reasons for taking part in the plot to assassinate the archduke. "Through him, I wanted to revenge myself on those groups who oppress the Slavs. I thought that such vengeance would be an effective warning to the ruling circles."

Cubrilovic was sentenced to 16 years in prison, while Popovic received a sentence of 13 years. Danilo Ilic, 24 at the time of the crime, was sentenced to be hanged along with four others who had aided the assassins. Nine of the defendants were freed, while the rest received varying prison sentences.

After the trial was over, Princip was taken to Theresienstadt, an old fortress north of Prague in the present-day Czech Republic. Life in the cold, rough prison was hard. Princip's shackles weighed 22 pounds (9.9 kg), and he was locked away, alone, in an unheated cell.

Only three of the six key assassins lived until the end of the war. Cubrilovic and Popovic were released from prison after Austria-Hungary collapsed in 1918. Mehmedbasic also outlived his fellow assassins.

Danilo Ilic died on February 3, 1915, hanged as a punishment for his crimes. On January 23, 1916, Cabrinovic died in prison from tuberculosis,

A plaque and a red rose mark the spot where Franz Ferdinand and Sophie were murdered.

an infectious disease that most often affects the lungs but that can attack almost any part of the body. Someone who saw him before his death said he looked like "a ghost." In February 1916, Trifko Grabez also died in prison from tuberculosis.

In early 1918, Princip became ill. Princip had probably been suffering from tuberculosis of the bones and joints even before he entered prison. Doctors amputated his arm, but the young man could not be saved. He died in a hospital bed on April 28, 1918.

Princip's body was taken in the dark of night from the hospital and buried in a secret grave. Later, however, a soldier revealed where the body was buried, and it was dug up and reburied with the others who took part in the Sarajevo assassination.

Princip did not live to see his dream of a Slavic nation realized. Before he died, a guard told him that the war that he had helped to start was tearing apart the Slavic nations. Belgrade, Serbia's capital, had just fallen to Austro-Hungarian troops. Princip insisted: "Serbia may be invaded but not conquered. Serbia will one day create Yugoslavia, mother of all South Slavs."

In 1929, 11 years after Princip's death, the nation of Yugoslavia was created from the kingdom of Serbs, Croats, and Slovenes, which had formed after the war. The country would remain a separate nation until World War II. In 1945, socialist Yugoslavia was created with six republics.

In Yugoslavia, Princip was viewed as a freedom fighter—someone who took action for the nation's independence. In Sarajevo, the street where Franz Ferdinand and Sophie were killed was renamed in Princip's honor, and a plaque and concrete footsteps marked the spot where he committed his crime. In 1953, a museum to honor him was opened, and his birthplace was made a national landmark. In 1992, during Bosnia's war against Serbia, Princip's reputation suffered, and he became despised as a terrorist. His museum was closed, and bombs destroyed his home.

By killing Franz Ferdinand, the young Bosnian assassins hoped to create sympathy for the cause of a united Serbian state. But they never expected their actions to cause a world war. Said Cabrinovic, "If I would have known what was going to happen, I would have sat down on these bombs and let them tear me to pieces." ◖

Timeline

December 2, 1848

Franz Josef becomes emperor of the Austrian empire.

December 18, 1863

Archduke Franz Ferdinand Erzherzog Von Osterreich-este is born in Austria.

February 8, 1867

Austria-Hungary is created when Franz Josef allows Hungary to have self-government within the empire.

July 1878

The Turks are driven out of the Balkans, and Austria-Hungary is granted temporary control of Bosnia and Herzegovina.

January 30, 1889

Crown Prince Rudolf commits suicide at Mayerling.

1894

Franz Ferdinand meets lady-in-waiting Sophie Chotek von Chotkova und Wognin.

July 1894

Gavrilo Princip is born in Obljaj, Bosnia.

May 19, 1896

Franz Ferdinand's father dies, making Franz Ferdinand heir to the throne of Austria-Hungary.

July 1, 1900

Franz Ferdinand and Sophie Chotek marry.

October 6, 1908

Austria-Hungary annexes Bosnia and Herzegovina.

May 9, 1911

The terrorist group known as the Black Hand is formed.

1912–1913

The Balkan Wars rip apart the region.

March 1914

Gavrilo Princip begins planning the assassination of Franz Ferdinand.

June 4, 1914

Princip and his helpers return to Sarajevo from Belgrade, Serbia.

June 23, 1914

Franz Ferdinand and Sophie depart from their castle in Bohemia for their trip to Sarajevo.

June 25, 1914

Franz Ferdinand arrives in Ilidza to meet Sophie.

June 27, 1914

Franz Ferdinand telegraphs Franz Josef to say he will leave Sarajevo the following day; Franz Ferdinand and Sophie attend formal dinner with Sarajevo's wealthiest and most powerful residents.

June 28, 1914

10 A.M.

Franz Ferdinand and Sophie arrive in Sarajevo for a reception at the city hall.

10:15 A.M.

Nedeljko Cabrinovic tosses a bomb at the archduke's car, wounding people in the following car as well as several bystanders.

10:45 A.M.

Moments after leaving city hall, the archduke and his wife are assassinated by Gavrilo Princip.

June 29, 1914

Riots break out in Sarajevo against Bosnian Serbs.

July 3, 1914

The funeral for the royal couple is held in Vienna.

July 23, 1914

Austria-Hungary issues an impossible ultimatum to Serbia.

July 25, 1914

Serbia refuses to comply with two of the items in the ultimatum.

July 28, 1914

Austria-Hungary declares war on Serbia.

July 30, 1914

Russia mobilizes its troops along the Austro-Hungarian and German borders.

August 1, 1914

Germany declares war on Russia.

Timeline

August 3, 1914

Germany declares war on France.

October 12, 1914

The trial against the assassins begins in Sarajevo.

October 29, 1914

Five of the six conspirators are found guilty of treason and murder.

February 3, 1915

Danilo Ilic is hanged in prison for his crimes.

January 23, 1916

Nedeljko Cabrinovic dies in prison from tuberculosis.

February 1916

Trifko Grabez dies in prison from tuberculosis.

April 28, 1918

Gavrilo Princip dies in prison from tuberculosis.

November 11, 1918

World War I ends at 11 A.M.

January 12–20, 1919

The Paris Peace Conference finalizes treaties for the defeated nations.

On the Web

For more information on this topic, use FactHound.

1 Go to *www.facthound.com*

2 Type in this book ID: 0756538572

3 Click on the *Fetch It!* button.

FactHound will find the best Web sites for you.

Historic Sites

Schloss Artstetten
A-366 Artstetten
Austria

This is the family home and burial place of Franz Ferdinand and Sophie and the home of the Archduke Franz Ferdinand Museum.

National World War I Museum
100 W. 26th St.
Kansas City, MO 64108-4616
816/784-1918

The official World War I museum of the United States honors those who served in World War I. It shows the results of World War I and how they impact the world today.

Look for More Books in This Series

The Berlin Airlift:
Breaking the Soviet Blockade

Black Tuesday:
Prelude to the Great Depression

The Hundred Days Offensive:
The Allies' Push to Win World War I

Kristallnacht, The Night of Broken Glass:
Igniting the Nazi War Against Jews

89

A complete list of **Snapshots in History** titles is available on our Web site: *www.compasspointbooks.com*

Glossary

annexed
claimed authority over the land of another nation

archduke
prince in the Austro-Hungarian empire

Balkans
countries on the Balkan Peninsula in southeastern Europe

Black Hand
Serbian terrorist group formed to oppose Austrian influence in the Balkans

Croats
people from Croatia, a country in the Balkans in southeastern Europe

federation
union of countries or states in which each country retains control of its own internal affairs

Habsburg
Austro-Hungarian royal family

imperial
pertaining to an empire

lady-in-waiting
woman appointed to wait upon a queen or princess

monarchy
type of government in which a king or queen is the head of state

Muslim
follower of the religion of Islam

Narodna Odbrana
"National Defense;" a Serbian group that opposed the Austrian annexation of Bosnia and Herzegovina

nationalist
someone who has a strong sense of nationalism, pride, and love of one's native country

noble
person with a high hereditary rank

oppressors
people who treat others harshly in order to keep them down

Ottoman Empire
Turkish empire that existed from the late 1200s until the end of World War I

propaganda
information spread to try to influence the thinking of people; often not completely true or fair

province
defined territory within a country that has its own identity, separate from but still a part of the larger country; similar to a state of the United States

Serbs
people from Serbia, a country in the Balkans in southeastern Europe

Slav
one of a group of peoples in eastern, southeastern, and central Europe, including Russians, Bulgars, Serbs, Croats, and Slovacks

subversive
someone who tries to overthrow a government

treason
crime of betraying one's country

ultimatum
final proposition, demand, or condition

Source Notes

Chapter 1

Page 10, line 21: Joachim Remak. *Sarajevo: The Story of a Political Murder.* New York: Criterion Books, 1959, p. 154.

Page 11, line 6: Ibid., p. 157.

Page 12, line 4: "When Sarajevo Triggered a War." *Time.com*, 30 Jan. 1984. 2 March 2007, www.time.com/time/magazine/article/0,9171,954101,00.html

Page 14, line 8: Ibid.

Page 14, line 25: "When Sarajevo Triggered a War."

Page 14, line 30: Lavender Cassels. *The Archduke and the Assassin.* Briarcliff Manor, N.Y.: Stein and Day, 1984, p. 179.

Chapter 2

Page 21, line 14: *The Archduke and the Assassin*, p. 54.

Page 21, line 22: André Gerolymatos. *The Balkan Wars: Conquest, Revolution, and Retribution from the Ottoman Era to the Twentieth Century and Beyond.* New York: Basic Books, 2002, p. 9.

Page 23, line 19: *The Archduke and the Assassin*, p. 22.

Page 24, line 15: Ibid., p. 43.

Page 24, line 27: *Sarajevo: The Story of a Political Murder*, p. 18.

Page 26, line 27: Ibid., p. 25.

Chapter 3

Page 32, lines 3 and 29: *The Archduke and the Assassin*, pp. 70 and 90.

Page 34, line 3: *Sarajevo: The Story of a Political Murder*, p. 27.

Chapter 4

Page 38, line 4: Ibid., p. 45.

Page 39, sidebar: "The Constitution of the Ujedinjenje ili Smrt: Unification or Death." *World War I Document Library online.* 1 March 2007. http://net.lib.byu.edu/~rdh7/wwi/1914m/blk-cons.htm

Page 39, line 10: *Sarajevo: The Story of a Political Murder*, p. 52

Page 41, line 1: *The Archduke and the Assassin*, p. 76.

Page 45, line 7: *Sarajevo: The Story of a Political Murder*, p. 76.

Chapter 5

Page 48, line 13: *The Archduke and the Assassin*, p. 162.

Page 49, line 3: *Sarajevo: The Story of a Political Murder,* p. 37.

Page 51, lines 3 and 21: Ibid., pp. 39 and 40.

Page 53, sidebar: Joseph M. Baernreither and Joseph Redlich. *Fragments of a Political Diary.* New York: Macmillan and Co., Limited, 1930, p. 11.

Page 54, line 3: Ibid., p. 106

Page 55, line 6: Ibid., p. 109.

Source Notes

Chapter 6

Page 60, line 14: "One Morning in Bosnia." *Time.com*, 3 July 1939. 2 March 2007, www.time.com/time/magazine/article/0,9171,761580-2,00.htm

Page 62, line 2: David DeVoss. "Searching for Gavrilo Princip." *Smithsonian*, August 2000, pp. 42–53. 10 Feb. 2007. http://w3.salemstate.edu/~cmauriello/pdf_his102/ princips.pdf

Page 63, line 2: *Sarajevo: The Story of a Political Murder*, p. 151.

Page 64, line 5: Ibid., p. 155.

Chapter 7

Page 68, line 3: "U.S. Ambassador's Reaction to Austria's Ultimatum, July 1914." *FirstWorldWar.com*. 14 Feb. 2007. www.firstworldwar.com/source/usreaction.html

Page 71, line 1: *The Archduke and the Assassin*, p. 184.

Page 73, line 3: "Germany's 'Blank Cheque' to Austria-Hungary, 6 July 1914." *FirstWorldWar.com*. 1 March 2007. www.firstworldwar.com/source/blankcheque.html

Page 73, line 18: "Austrian Ministerial Council Meeting Minutes, 7 July 1914." *FirstWorldWar.com*. 26 Feb. 2007. www.firstworldwar.com/source austriancouncilmeeting.html

Page 74, line 4: "Austrian Ultimatum to Serbia, 23 July 1914." FirstWorldWar.com. 8 March 2007. www.firstworldwar.com/source/austrianultimatum.html

Page 75, line 9: "Austria-Hungary's Declaration of War with Serbia, 28 July 1914." FirstWorldWar.com. 8 March 2007. www.firstworldwar.com/source/ autrohungariandeclarationofwar_serbia.htm

Page 75, sidebar: "The Willy-Nicky Telegrams." *World War I Document Library online*. 8 March 2007. http://net.lib.byu.edu/~rdh7/wwi/1914/willynilly.html

Chapter 8

Page 81, lines 1 and 12: *Sarajevo: The Story of a Political Murder*, pp. 214 and 222.

Page 82, line 4: *The Archduke and the Assassin*, p.148

Page 82, line 13: "Cabrinovic, Nedjelko." *World War I Document Library online*. 10 March 2007. http://net.lib.byu.edu/~rdh7/wwi/bio/c/cabrinov.html

Page 82, line 17: *Sarajevo: The Story of a Political Murder*, p. 245.

Page 83, sidebar: Ibid., p. 94.

Page 85, line 3: David DeVoss. "Searching for Gavrilo Princip." *Smithsonian*, August 2000, pp. 42–53. http://w3.salemstate.edu/~cmauriello/pdf_his102/princips.pdf

Page 85, line 28: *Sarajevo: The Story of a Political Murder*, p. 222.

SELECT BIBLIOGRAPHY

Brook-Shepherd, Gordon. *Archduke of Sarajevo: The Romance and Tragedy of Franz Ferdinand of Austria*. Boston: Little, Brown and Company, 1984.

Cassels, Lavender. *The Archduke and the Assassin*. Briarcliff Manor, N.Y.: Stein and Day, 1984.

Cornwall, Mark (ed.). *The Last Years of Austria-Hungary*. Exeter, U.K.: University of Exeter Press, 2002.

Fromkin, David. *Europe's Last Summer*. New York: Alfred A. Knopf, 2004.

Owings, W.A. Dolph. *The Sarajevo Trial, Volumes I and II*. Chapel Hill, N.C.: Documentary Publications, 1984.

FURTHER READING

Adams, Simon. *World War I*. New York: DK Publishing, 2007.

Ross, Stewart. *Assassination in Sarajevo: The Trigger for World War I*. Chicago: Heinemann Library, 2006.

Woolf, Alex. *Assassination in Sarajevo*. Austin, Texas: Raintree Steck-Vaughn, 2003.

Ziff, John. *Causes of World War I*. Stockton, N.J.: OTTN Publishing, 2005.

Index

ABOUT THE AUTHOR

Robin S. Doak is a writer of nonfiction books for children. She lives with her husband and two children on the coast of Maine.

IMAGE CREDITS

AKG-Images pp. **11** and **87**, **22** and **86**, **31**, **42**, **52**, **67** and **87**, **77**; Alamy pp. **61** (Juergen Hasenkopf), **84** (snappdragon); The Bridgeman Art Library p. **41** (Peter Newark American Pictures); Corbis **cover** and p. **9**, pp. **15**, **33** and **86**, **50**, **54**, **64**, **78** and **87** (Bettmann), **12–13** (Rykoff Collection), **17** and **86** (Fine Art Photographic Library), **20** (Austrian Archives), **29** (Alinari Archives), **37** (Stefano Bianchetti), **6** and **68**, **71**, **72** (Hulton-Deutsch Collection); Getty Images pp. **25** (Imagno/Austrian Archives), **2** and **81** and **88**, **34**, **44**, **49**, (Hulton Archive), **47**, **57** (Roger Viollet Collection), **5** and **62–63** (Time & Life Pictures); Topfoto p. **38**.